MAPLAND

Also by Gary Allen

Poetry
Irish Notes
The Farthest Circle
Mending Churches
Making Waves
Languages
Exile
North of Nowhere
Iscariot's Dream
The Bone House
The Next Room
Ha, Ha
White Lines
Mexico
Jackson's Corner

Short Stories
Introductions

Novels
Cillin
The Estate
Twenty-Eight Worlds

MAPLAND

POEMS

by Gary Allen

CLEMSON UNIVERSITY PRESS

Copyright 2016 by Clemson University
ISBN 978-1-942954-31-6

Published by Clemson University Press in Clemson, South Carolina

Editorial Assistant: Sam Martin and Kara McKlemurry

Cover design by Charis Chapman

To order copies, please visit the Clemson University Press website: www.clemson.edu/press.

Contents

Acknowledgments • viii

Part 1: Dreamland

Two Women Sitting Down • 2
The Kiss • 4
Slogans • 5
Two Doors • 6
Self Portrait at One Second • 7
The Smoothing-Iron • 8
The Ambassadors • 9
Christ Among the Doctors • 11
Poet and Star • 13
The Rooks • 14
Loerke's Horse • 15
The Wheel • 17
Up the Arbor • 18
A Better Life • 19
Walking to Lubeck • 20
Pit of Bones • 21
Golem • 22
Seghers Courtyard • 23
Baal • 25
The Key to my Aunt's House • 26
Eureka • 27
Witches of Hawaii • 28

Part 2: Compasses

Dog Meat • 32
On the Nature of Hanging • 33
And We Walked to Budapest • 35
Milking-parlour • 36
Ohio • 37
Carson's Table • 38

Characters Without a Stage • 40
Swine • 42
At the Movies • 43
Queer • 44
The Space White • 46
How I Joined the Communist Party of Ireland • 47
The Holding Company • 48

Part 3: Pathways

When You Are Old • 50
The Examination Board • 51
The Wide Blue Yonder • 52
The May King • 53
The Child • 54
Letter from the Republic of London • 55
Two Blue Moons • 56
Remember • 58
The Blow Fly • 59
The First Day of Creation • 60
John L. Burns • 61
On Watching Men Cut Down a Tree • 63
Star Man • 64
A Pair of Praying Hands • 65
Inside Out • 66
Mapland • 67
Huguenot • 69

Part 4: Mile Stones

How I Discovered Livingstone • 72
The Zoo • 73
Bach • 74
Narcissus • 75
Sibyl • 77
Fishing Upper Silesia • 78
Kite • 79
The Running Man • 80

The Piano Player • 81
Path • 82
Shlomo • 84
Kafka's Travelling Corpse • 85
Don Quixote and Sancho Panza • 86
Five Points • 87
The Rising Sun • 89
Bukowski • 90
Concrete Cows • 92
Xenophanes in Hell • 93

About the Poet • 94

Acknowledgments

Some of these poems have been published in the following literary journals: *Acumen, Agenda, Ambit, Antigonish Review, Australian Book Review, Existere, FourXFour, Glasgow Review of Books, Hesa, Poetry and Audience, Poetry NZ, The Reader, The Shop, The South Carolina Review, The Stinging FLy, Westerly, The Yellow Nib*, and the anthology *Best Australian Poems 2015.*

Part 1

Dreamtime

Two Women Sitting Down

You can almost taste the burning earth
as it blows away
grit between your teeth and tongue –

up here in the North, near Bootu Creek
everything is ochre red and brown
a moonscape

two women sitting down, as if for a rest
but you have to look hard
to see it through ancient eyes
you have to *dream* it into existence

like my friend out in the West
who is looking for help to hold it all together
couldn't even nail a screen door to a jamb
couldn't even keep a wife
the dust and sand making sacred mounds
on the tables in the back office
the animals gone feral.

It must have been away back
when these two fat ladies took a breather
from the heat and the flies
and never got up again, what was the point?

They remind me of my mother and aunt
overweight like some poor people are
they were always sitting about somewhere
pretending to smoke
as if waiting for a better world to go by

until they died, none the wiser
became inanimate like rock
who'll remember them?
not even above ground –
in dreamtime everything is upside down

and impregnated with meaning
a rock, a bird, a painting
before we came, before we go again:
and did they bury you up to your pretty brown heads
in the sand,
and then kick them from your shoulders?
laughing like kookaburras
guffawing like heavy road machinery.

These two women sitting down are very tired now
a million manganese sunsets have passed them by
a pile of washing on the sideboard
the school books waiting to be backed with wallpaper
the children hand in hand waiting at the country station
and the understanding,
that all women sacrifice their children to the world.

The Kiss

Death has two faces:
a clapboard house by the sea
surrounded by fields of wheat

where I found you hanging
worn like a thin brown penny –
you had a pathological fear of death
you found it in loneliness

the rodent marks crisscrossing the dust
they jumped from the orange boxes to feed
the low murmur of the sea, the wheat heads, the flies
brought me here
the last bus-stop from Alkmaar.

I knew you were angry, my love –
the calls stopped, the letters incoherent with venom
stopped.

Your grandmother was an informer
shot and left as a warning by the footbridge
every morning her own mother
combed her red hair and talked to her about the farm
the embarrassment of her naked bruised skin:

then the ambulance and the hearse came
and the policemen in their funny uniforms –
they asked me if I knew you?
I said no, I was only walking in the dunes
with a dog I didn't own.

Death has two faces –
a mother telling her daughter
that she is going to tie her hair back
she couldn't see the red hole in the nape of her neck
or the breath that had stopped

and the sand, and the inverted nipple
and the stubborn afternoon
and the people who came and went
and would go and live their continuous lives
like friezes on a temple wall.

SLOGANS

And the house depressed me immediately
all too familiar
that smell of closed-in damp places
the rotting wood pulling away from the window frames
the greasy linoleum kitchen, the echo of water drips
the animal-fat stink of cooking, and drying dish cloths
the small grates full of burnt rubbish.

And I knew the narrow creaking staircase
the pokey bedrooms always dim
religious pictures on the walls
the brown stains of family photographs removed
the small paned windows looking over
jagged bottle-topped stone walls
and factories, and church halls, and outside lavatories.

Who have lived here like lice for two hundred years?
growing old like brickwork
chipped away by a form of stunted living?
I know them too, as much a part of the house
as a street of suchlike houses
and children sick with lung and chest complaints
the second-hand prams and carrycots in the hallway.

I thought all this had ended with my childhood
that poverty had somehow gone away
but like political violence, it stinks the drains
the hardboard nailed to the inside of the front door
the smashed and splintered wood
the buckets of water and old blankets kept near the windows –

then Jozef sighs, and shows me
the almost childish scrawl of slogans
slapdash and soot-blackened on the outside of the house.

Two Doors

You go through two doors
leaving behind a cardboard suitcase
marked with chalk –

it could be the dock lights of Belfast
in an early morning Lough mist
or something more, a Black Sea port?
Yalta, perhaps?

My father, and mother, and sister
are like children again
holding hands
moving through the long grasses of meadows
I think I remember
through grass that grows strangely.

Tildarg is in my head –
it is a tune
my father whistled it high like a fife –
my father was a stony field:

when I stayed on the Rue de l'Ecole
I bought a menorah from a book shop on the Seine
then, agonizing over its history
and where it might have come from,
I went back and bought the other.

Is it true? that nothing exists
but atoms and empty space?

My father shrugs
my father, and mother, and sister
sit like angry lifeless granite columns:

the dead are gone, the dead are soon forgotten
they bring us poems that are incomprehensible
they suffer us, as God must too.

Self Portrait at One Second

I was born looking out
across a barracks wasteland of frozen ice
if there was any colour in the monotone grey and white and black
it was a red streak of sunlight
weak like a child's eye.

I was a boxer, a priest
depending on which lover looked down
upon my snub face on the pillow
depending on how they would regret
knowing me in a later life

as I spoke to them only through the iron of a grill
and broke them into forgiveness
so that no man would ever be the same.

This poet sucked at fingers and chewed bread
before he could make rivers and bones
out of words that were beaten in

take poor Durer, he made himself into a woodcut
with all the pomp and circumstance of a loser
but how else could he present a true image of himself?

I was born a loser, I was born outside the womb
I was born into a time of men in great coats
no poet dubbed our door with infant blood
or cut the earth like a dumb farmer
or defecated in a bucket in a room full of orphan boys.

This work is not pretty, they said
no woman will love its coldness
or raise a spark to give it life
but if you find the still space between the door
and the outside wall, the hot-water bottles
and the secondhand bureau
you might see me fleetingly on the hard ground
they call the Hollow.

The Smoothing-iron

Ghost girl, my sister white
and sickly, sitting on the edge of the narrow bed

she has lost all sense of being, her mask face
tracked with broken adolescence
she is tired, even after sleep
her white work blouse immaculate
yet her arms are tattooed with iron burns.

I hate to see her submissive to an adult world
she was not known for coming through doors lightly
disturbing the father of the house
writing sermons against the Catholic Church.

The street lights are still on
the younger children are at the table
still sleeping, they try to chew bread,
I am in service, she tells this world with resignation:

Munch is pulling oars across the inlet
to a stony beach and a wooden clapboard chalet
the confusion of colours are already in his head
mistresses are like larch trees
silver-stripping the foreshores of his mind.

My sister coughs into the sink
and pulls on the coat her father saved to buy
as she leaves the house, she is a painting
an expression of blood and desires –
she wants to be a mistress to all the gentlemen
promenading their wives along the smoothing-iron.

The Ambassadors

In all the shop windows are little devils dancing –
I feel oppressed in a foreign country
in half an hour the lights go on
in half an hour millions will be coming home from work
no one can see the children's faces
no one can see the washing on the lines
sulphur hangs in yellow clouds around the drains

and guns are easy to come by, as easy as fireworks
what about the three Irish boys who were dissolved in a bath of acid?
or that kid who hanged himself from a motorway bridge
because no one would employ him
because he felt worthless
because he had no girlfriend?

I see the secret pointers to my life's end everywhere
like the one lane closed that morning just outside Arnhem
the chestnut brown horse that had made a dash for it
lying on its side, soaked with the rain, its own blood and shit
great legs and flank jerking in its death throes –

and the traffic continued, like paper planes
names and signs for the industrial estates of Germany
or through Belgium to Paris and the South:
Europe has lost its way, Europe means nothing
look at Spain, Greece, Ireland.

Exactly a year ago, I was summoned back –
on the carriageway up from Dublin
to the hospital in the North
each of us encased, lonely in our metaphysical minds
the bleak October fields and dreary housing estates
where people were waking up to their own imminent deaths

out of nowhere, down a slip road
the travellers came in their ponies and traps
laughing wildly, in and out through the early traffic
only boys really, in their mullets and designer jeans
until the next exit, and then they were gone, just as sudden.

All the ghosts are out this evening
reflected in the mirrors of the shop windows
and now I am older, nothing ever is as it seems
like the film I watched on Dutch T.V.
a slow moving camera skimming from above
the frozen wastes of the Arctic
while deep down, the permafrost is millions of years old
like a soul, like a heart, and still forming.

The dead are with us this evening too
their voices garbled on the telegraph-wires –
I have seen too much of Europe
too many statues, tapestries, cathedrals
medieval ruins sitting like old portraits
like Schiller's ghost

on high crags, and river bends:
Europe is an anachronism
where the human soul is worthless –
even the children are born old
collecting coins, in their cloaks and hats
cynical, arrogant, secretive, like Holbein's Ambassadors.

Christ among the Doctors

And what have we here Mr. D?
it could be a girl with an oval face
rather than a gifted boy of twelve
being administered to by a leech
a simpleton whose mouth protrudes downwards
she/he could be telling him anything about a flat world
is truth infallible? is there a fundamental way
of knotting the strands of any truth together
to form a flat exact picture of the universe
of what is inside each of us?

Oh to be the proverbial fly on history's wall
the vastness of the temple, the death bed
what questions did he ask? what answers given?
or was it the mundane dry-stick rhetoric
that comes with religious instruction
by dried-out old men so clever with age
they have forgotten how fresh it is to be wrong?

like the catechisms I learned on a Saturday night
for an auld fart in a cheap sober suit
who bribed God with Scottish toffees
who slapped a child's face hard with every wrong answer.

Grow up in the sticks, brought up with the stick:
my earliest memory of a church, was thirst
and the smell of man's timeless dust
the scorpion truth that waited everywhere to trap you –
keep silent, little girl/boy, these doctors are older than you think
and keep a stock of timber and nails
they can wait, hooded eye-lids crusted with pustules
won't stop them seeing, that to know the truth about everything
is the greatest sin, is playing at being a proud God.

We can make a good guess at what was said inside the temple
but do we really want to know?
after all these years? after we have put so many to the sword?
hacked our way through the softness to get to the tough nut?
made children learn it all over and over again by rote

so that they hated the thin-lipped bibles
and the shitty righteousness of the teacher
who had given-up his Sunday morning lie-in:
I like to think anyway, that when Jesus
the girl/boy came outside to the sun
he must have thought, What a waste,
these doctors have only murder in mind.

POET AND STAR

There is only one star shining in the sky
this late November afternoon
bright enough to be a searchlight
on the humped and huddled backs lining-up
between three rows of specially commissioned buses
beyond the compounds and the wire and the high gates
boiler-suits, donkey jackets, combat coats
and the poet who is distant, but part among them
is the only one who watches the star hover

above the woods and the castle and the industrial complex
and the council housing-estate, and the columns
of army trucks moving into the country lanes
to take-up positions for the evening.

I am sitting four rows behind the poet
who isn't really a poet yet
but feels the coming darkness
and the branches pressing against the bus windows
and there is my friend, he would die soon after
a tout, they botched his punishment and he bled to death
and the boy with the red hair whose name I can't remember
came out of army interrogation, and hanged himself
from a motorway bridge.

The town is sleepy tonight, too quiet
the shops closed early, weighted barrels
and wire mesh outside the public houses
soon the security-gates would be locked
and the star will rise high
above the drawn curtains and the television sets.

How can I tell him that nothing in this world
ever really changes, like the star from a billion years ago
that life is just as indifferent and mercenary
and the future forgets the living and the dead

who have achieved nothing in their short spans:
I hope the poet, against all of the world's odds,
becomes a poet, for then, he will have hurled himself
against the stream.

The Rooks

When man was a shadow upon a young earth
the rooks came
covering a sulphurous sky
sound before language
they scavenged the land

and survived, the forests felled
they found common roosting in isolated coppices
manse grounds
the peripheral of towns and golf-course rough

unchanged in their ways
almost since the beginning of time
tied into the destiny of the landscape
the interface of wandering souls:

coming home through the woods at dusk
the light leaving a darkening sky
the dry leaves rattling into the burn

there is a sudden cacophony of noise
and the quick rush of wings
as the rooks rise deafeningly into the air

and I am reminded in my wonderment
of the oldness of this world
and the pre-history of everything
the endurance of the rooks.

Loerke's horse

Loerke's horse is a muscular upright stallion
Loerke's horse is pre-war German
its fifteen hands reduced to a miniature bronze

its large frame has pulled carts all its life
and now it is sure of its strength
an unchained modern Prometheus, it snorts the cold air.

Loerke has suffered too
a woman with a child that is not his
sits in the recess by the chimney breast
singing with hunger
in a block of flats that is only cement dust
rotten cross beams, blackened windows
like one of Loerke's giant granite friezes

he has carried children on hand-carts
from the hospital to the crematorium:
when he was only a child himself, after school
he would torch the makeshift huts
under the bridge spans along the Elbe

this is his will to power
that he can harness the suffering around him
work it into a world dominated by industry.

Leitner says he is haughty and loathes people
especially women, Leitner is large like a great sculpture
a fair young man who is unwilling, either naïve or indifferent –
like his lovemaking.

Loerke is called a dwarf by the kids
yes, his clothes are dirty
his beret is out of shape
but his mind is sharp, and he knows how to get under
the skin, he has learned that the world for modern man
will be cruel and unforgiving
money makes no difference, can only buy humiliation
that death is the sound of boots in corridors
of not being on the ball, like foreigners.

Mapland

The young girl is naked and barely formed
sitting astride the powerful horse
her weak legs clutching its quivering flanks
someone he has loved, and tortured, and controlled?
Still, this is no Przewalski horse, but a tamed resentful monster.

The Wheel

So what do you do when the dream is over
you make great preparations to build a boat
that can carry crew, munitions, dried rations
a boat strong enough, made from hard wood
ferried down from the North with spices and gold
a boat fleeting and short hulled, that can race
the rapids, glide the sluggish pebbled bed
turn easily in mid-river, manoeuvre mud and sand banks

and lazy bends, with shelter from the torturous sun
the biting hail, the treacherous winds
from the great desert plains, and set sail
for now that He is dead and the impossible dream
of conquest from ocean to ocean is as fatuous
as the men fat and languid with many native wives,
what else is there to do, but journey

the long days on still water, passing mangroves
and lone stupas with writing none of us
has ever seen, or could understand
like the hot wind and water crumbling the mud away
to leave the most perfect grid
of long lost cities that had been buried aeons before

the oars plying the dirty water where vultures
and tattooed naked men come to drink and bathe
or simply stare at the crazy Yavanas going nowhere
with such determination, or to shower the boat
with long tipped ineffectual arrows –
there is no civilization, every man lives
one small piece of eternity that ends at its source
like a wheel, where we must come upon one another's footprint.

Up the Arbor

Let us gather round and watch –
a Saturday afternoon, better than the professional wrestling
or the winners at Newmarket or Newcastle
this Sisyphean family, dysfunctional on the green
where they have moved scuffed settees and armchairs
and a light-stand, into the open on the Buttershaw estate
are passionately cursing their way through
a kitchen-sink drama, a passion play of sorts.

The father in string-vest (of course) is fighting drunk
and racist, but one must ask oneself,
does he really understand he is racist?
anymore than the Asian youth comes from Pakistan:

as the last of the winter light closes down the moors
the residents are standing around in small nervous groups
but aren't sure if they are being insulted
or are the product of another social experiment
or the product of a creative-writing class
or the characters come to life
from one of their own's imagination –
one more teenage pregnancy.

The washing is on the lines
the children are horse-riding their Christmas Chopper bikes
Jameel has gone to fight in Belfast
and in The Beacon, Andrea is lying
on the piss covered toilet floor
quietly haemorrhaging in the brain –
and the play will soon be over
and we can get on with being forgotten.

A BETTER LIFE

Karina has a rented flat on the Crumlin Road
she doesn't understand the politics
she doesn't always understand the insults
but she has three jobs, she cleans offices in the morning
works as a checkout girl, then cleans in the evening
when she comes home she is exhausted, she is forty years old
then she goes to her English lessons at night school.
Karina has varicose veins from standing long hours
and is waiting for an operation, her daughter
is fifteen and lives with her father in Latvia
Karina misses her, and sometimes home
and she is tired and in pain all the time
and there is never enough money, especially now
her friend Anton has come to stay
he is terminally ill and can't work
or get benefits, he isn't expected
to live much longer, but is always smiling
and her friend Ivanda was beaten-up
by her husband and needs somewhere to stay –
what can she do? and the local kids
are wild and paint slogans on her windows.
Karina is seeing a man from the Civil Service
whom she met through the internet, they walk in the parks
and eat sandwiches, when she can get time off
but everyone needs her now, she texts angrily,
I want to go home, I want to be with my child
but I am working hard every day like a horse with bad legs.

Walking to Lubeck

When Johann walked the four-hundred kilometres
from Luneburg to Lubeck
was he thinking about Buxtehude's daughter
or the abendmusiken at the Marienkirche
or its great organ, or the leather that had worn thin

on the unsurfaced, sandy road
as he made his way through the heath land and woods
stopping off in small villages where the peasants were as dumb
as the animals they herded to slaughter

until he reached Lubeck, with its narrow crowded lanes
and passageways, the flute towers
and the brick gothic architecture of the Marienkirche
an island within an island of the Trave

or did he think of his parents' unmarked graves in Eisenach
the snow like tiny cantatas playing upon the earth –
only months apart? or was he thinking about the cudgel mark
across his brow?

On his journey back to Luneburg
after three unofficial months
he lay down on the cold Luneburg heath
and had a dream, or a vision –

in the dark sky, he saw an arrow and a cross
and a machine of some sort
like carts end to end, but travelling at great speed without horses
across the countryside, full of wretched people in strange clothes

Budapest, Budapest, its great metallic wheels seemed to wail
ungamlager, the word had no meaning to him
and then it was gone, leaving him awed and fearful.

When he told Buxtehude of this vision much later,
he asked his now friend and mentor what he thought it meant?
Buxtehude thought long and hard
and then answered, It means dear Johann
that the German people will be exalted above all
by means of their music and intellect.

Pit of Bones

In this natural cave shaft
the bones of bears and humans have been thrown
but there are no marks on them
from either weapons or teeth
no one has made sacrifice or ornament from them
to blow through or necklace

and time has passed away in its emptiness
here in Northern Spain
the same wind, and rain, and parching sun burning down
that reaches me on my Northern isle –

Bones are made to last a long time round here,
my father said, as though bones could talk or remember
who clothed them or put them here

his blue post-office suit
the cloth rubbed shiny
had seen both weddings and funerals
and sat out questioning in the Green Glens bar
where they asked him to spell his name
as though some Maori sailor
had tattooed it on his brow for all to see

Look, he told them with an ex-soldier's grit,
I am four-hundred years old, and forty-three feet
and planted here until I am called up

as the taxi waited on the Chapel Hill
before going down to his eldest daughter's wedding,
There is still time, the driver smoking laughed,
They do it differently down there –

all gone now, like a mirage that shimmers for a while
or a scrimshoner packing up his tools
or men bring up human and animal bones
brushing away the clay, measuring, cataloguing
trying to read their histories.

Golem

Judah Loew, it was not me who ran amok
murdering the rich merchants in their tall fancy houses
watching how man's life leaves his warm body
different to how I died on the eve of every Sabbath
the written shem forced from my voiceless mouth
and then returned to bring this Vltava clay back to life

to my unshaped form, an unfinished human being
before God's eyes –
no, it was *my* creator's will and power that fed it.
Look through these eyes, Judah Loew
while good men sleep, even in the Josefov

coughing children bungled together in their cots
these clay feet on the rickety stairs of slums
seeking out those you would have murdered
groping my way in human blindness through the squat
sharp angled, squinting buildings

seeing fleeting images that in a perpetual short life
have neither past nor future
yet hearing every breath, heart beat, rat gnawing
and scratching, from the Old Town Square
to the river, to the stones shifting in the cemeteries.

Unrequited love is like grief, Judah Loew
the failure to let go, and take one's rightful place:
each Friday night, I climbed the outside rungs
on the synagogue roof, to my deathbed attic
denied what is human or divine

so yes, Judah Loew, I cracked their necks
beneath my clay fingers, throttled them
in their quilted beds, and saw for a moment
in a mist of red, the true nature of the law,
of man and creature separated from God.

Seghers Courtyard

In my Master's house, everything has its place
five stories tall, if you include the attics and the basement
where we sleep, adjacent to the airing linen, the bags of spuds
the cold broken brickwork, the narrow staircases
and opaque thick glass of the windows
the glazed tiles of fireplaces and cooking hoods.

In the paved courtyard where we sit, shelling and peeling
on summer evenings, among the washing and the cats
where we talk of masters and crude sex
without really knowing either, though I share a cot
with Johanna whose hands wander, and whose tongue is hot

you don't need to see, but you can feel
the sailing boats glide the deeper canals
with goods that come from far off lands with strange people
and sometimes there is silence, like the vast emptiness
around the great pillars of the Oude Kerk.

I know a boy with blond hair like straw and thick lips
a butcher's apprentice from Zutphen
who follows me like a sniffing dog
along the tow path of bare trees and frozen solid water,
Come into the barren fields, he pleads with me

but he is of a different religion, and will die for that
like last summer, when stones were thrown
from barricades of wagons and household furniture
and buildings burned all through the city:
William came through this way on a great horse
with men in armour, and flags, and drums
on his way to do battle at Utrecht.

Johanna says the Catholics will not rest
till everyone of us is raped and murdered
but that we have strong friends and God's protection
Johanna wakened one night to see the devil standing by our cot
a dark man with red eyes, very well dressed, like a gentleman
who looked like Philip of Spain – where do you come from?

Mapland

she asked me once, on the shore beyond Zeeland
where my family harvested the waves and salted herring
no one goes back – there is a pear tree in my Master's courtyard
that never blossoms or bears fruit, but dips towards the water
and guards the locked door into a world unknown now,
A gilded cage, Johanna laughs,
where we are like two of my Master's little love birds.

Baal

Hunted across three states for setting fire to barns
as though he wanted to destroy the structures of the state
consume everything in flame, like his renegade soul
the small spark that sets off a conflagration
like the beginnings of a drunken ballad
the bales of hay, rolled like Johanna's hair
smouldering from the concertinaed inside, like glowing cigarette tips –

she drowned herself in the mill pond, after he had seduced her
the silly girl. Life is but a game of hide and seek
the click-click of billiard balls in the afternoon
the invalided men coming off the long trains
the heart attack that almost killed him
when he was twelve years old:

this is Baal, different coloured eyes, facial tic
bad teeth, a poet who sings of debauchery –
to make a myth of oneself, and finally believe it,
is that not where madness lies?

Poor Ekart, the suffering fool, knowing only coldness and hunger
he paints his little postcards, a pfennig a time
and died painfully, some say, by my hand.

Sing to me, The drowned girl, The dirty song,
Remembering Marie A –
this is the first play, my creator is as dumb as I am
as I lie here among the meadows, not more than a chalk circle
from where I was conceived in Augsburg

listening to the pile driver down the valley
alone among the pines, dying – not a word can be recalled today

even he can't remember me, tired old intellectual
with his weakness for flesh and causes
his belief that we are all brothers –
I am Baal, my voice will not diminish altogether
even to those I have betrayed.

The Key to My Aunt's House

The early morning sun slicing through the slats
of the exotic venetian blinds
brings good feeling and calm

on the heavy black silent phone
that doesn't ring
the electrical goods in the fitted kitchen
and the embossed wallpaper on the staircase and landing
the cocky hunter with the broke shotgun

in the crook of his arm
his legs crossed, backed against a sturdy oak
his hunting dogs and lady at his feet

white laminated doors leading to closets
and the imitation American car in the driveway –
her husband and his bad heart
on business in Ontario, wherever that is –

the noise of BT engineer's pneumatic drill
tennis players coming on to the courts
of the Lamont Gymnasium at the Technical College:

it is quiet here, the bunch of keys on the coffee table
lie heavily – the boys who threw stones at him
because his parents worshipped at a different church
who thought he had more than them
making him take flight like a hare,

are milling around the top of the cul-de-sac –
a child should be at school
knowing nothing of fear or death
but intuitively sensing
that this would be a good time and place to die,
like a hare that gives-up and shivers in the morning sun.

Eureka

The mines have moved North, over the years
like the retreating sea
leaving footprints hundreds of years old

something hangs around on the tail end of history
like a bad smell
like rotten vegetation, rotten socks and semmits

those who dig for diamonds, pan for gold
or unearth the bones of creatures they don't understand
will turn over and throw away to the slag heap
the minuscule of what once thrived here

the broken shards of once best crockery
clock and bed springs
that was carried with such care by the natives
from the exterior

dog nails, rusted bits of tools
and heavy lead cans, lead balls
scraps of faded photographs and Eureka badges –

that every man thinks he once meant something
that somehow they would be remembered
for the sweat of their brows
for what they built with their own hands
carved from the desert and the heat of the bush
for the principled and stand they took against tyranny

but the walls of hovels have tumbled in
grown through with weeds and scrub
the water towers squeak, the water gone
the farm implements saved for and bought through catalogues

are tossed somewhere in the far bush
the shored-up walls of the mines buckled outwards
there is no language, but the fierce sun

sometimes a naked, painted boy will appear
as if from nowhere, and nose around the once laid out rooms
toe the iron and bone of crazy men
and finding nothing of use to him, walk away again.

Witches of Hawaii

I was watching the ball players in Kapi'olani park
decked out in every colour imaginable
the oversized parents with their smoking barbecues
drinking alcohol from tins wrapped in brown paper bags
or from plastic cola bottles

and the sun like the heat was fierce
even under the leaves of the hau trees
so that the hardy vegetation on the slopes of Diamond Head
seemed to crackle, with the balls that arced into the blue:

there are no witches on Hawaii now
since the Americans came and drove them out
except for the Kahuna who beat the old man
to death with a bible
who saw the Haole bodies floating on the sea
like the silver upturned bodies of dead fish

and the enslavement of plantations
sandalwood, whaling stations, rum, religion
swapping war canoes for surf boards.

The Cardinals come up close
thinking they have no natural predators:
but the men were forced to live and work
on the sugar plantations
rolling the stems between logs
evaporating the sucrose, adding lime to purify
filling the large copper kettles with molasses

and at night, flying low like black bats
up on the cool highlands, the dark forests
of waterfalls, and craters, and caves
visiting the sleeping, sucking out their souls
long silk hair flowing out like water –

what we don't understand is evil, yet seductive
poor white-faced missionaries two months out from San Francisco
finding sin in the native nakedness and beliefs
like the sailors with their syphilis
and the quick deconstruction of a civilization

and Stevenson in the sea cool shade
sipping whiskey and writing out his years
listens to a story of the Hawaiian witch
who shrouded the island in ghostly mist
to stop the Haole finding it

but they did, ringing it with tunnels and gun emplacements
concreting its deep harbours
high rise hotels for tourists
who lie all day on the white beaches
or the marines who fight on volcano juice
or the Japanese who haunt the shopping malls
and wedding parlours –

and yet, in the evenings, when the hot wind catches
the tops of the palm trees, and really does sing
songs and voices you can't quite catch
I am reminded of miles of water surrounding us
and the hair's breadth touch of Hawaiian witches.

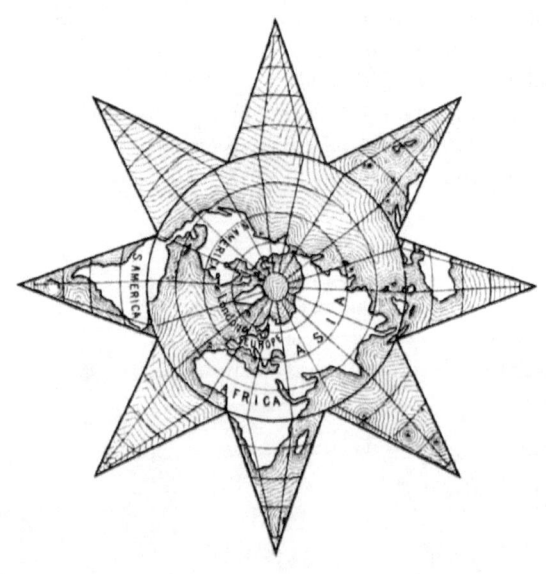

Part 2

Compasses

Dog Meat

Seven horses lie like bloated bear skins
dotted along South Carriage Drive
the hot wind that suddenly seared among them
cut away their legs.

The sirens talking to one another
the earthy stink of warm dung and burning
the farriers splashed from head to foot
with blood, the litter
of car wreckage, four and six inch nails.

England the bitch, the sow, the dumb
washes rosy red and mixed
into the drains

with little chunks of flesh
that cling to the bubbled tar
neither human nor equine

but a hybrid of historical letting
like windblown seeds in the air
and cloudy dust, that settles down to zero pain

like the Japanese tourists in the White Tower
and the black taxi cabs in the angry traffic
the cameras hoisted back on to BBC vans

and the shredded corpses covered with sheets
until they can be removed
and disposed off
like truth, like justice –
like an insurance salesman round the doors.

On the Nature of Hanging

Isn't it a strange way to end life
and yet perfectly poised and balanced
the voice cut off
the body needing just a fingertip to set it swinging.

Dogs or cats don't have the same finesse
their struggle too animal-dumb and violent
but humans have something majestic about them
even in their terror
even in suicide – hanging seems the king of death

not cowardly like poisoning
or messy like the coup de grace of the firing-squad
clinical like injections or gas

almost as if the human neck was made for it:
it's the comical contraptions we devise
to kill our fellow humans
like the soldiers who hung the Serbian men and women
on boards with ropes attached to their legs
pulled downwards by wooden levers stood on by Austrian boots

the short drop, the long drop, the pole
Black Jack's head coming away from his body
suspended from cranes in sport's stadiums
like crows on mass wires
like coats on the vast iron rail in Prazsky Hrad,
when the deed was done, the twitching over
they simply ran the body along the line
to join those rotting at the end, and so on.

And my mother said, when she was a child
on the day of a hanging up at the Crumlin
they were brought in from playing in front of the house
that everything went dark and silent
and all the birds stopped singing
like a long held breath
at what we were about to do under God's nose –
and try to get away with it.

Who was the first to hang?
why, it had to be Judas
the pain of betrayal gnawing away at his guts
thirty stupid pieces of silver he didn't really want
stringing himself up from a tree branch
in the potter's field, twenty minutes of strangulation
the bulging eyes, the blackened tongue
the creaking twists of ordinary rope
his feet spinning anticlockwise
through history ever since.

And We Walked to Budapest

And we walked to Budapest
mostly at night
a crust of black bread, a heel-print of muddy water
and although we were silent, we sang songs in our hearts
for the loved ones we were going to meet.

Fanni, I have written down my poems for you
should I die
in a red exercise book, like a school child
but poems of love
sung in the quarries and the copper mines
where hangings and whips structured time
and no one spoke of home.

We were happy once, were we not?
and art made everything possible
now the cobbled streets of Budapest
are lined with rows of little ones
like stacks of wood –
a jackboot on soft pomegranates.

We walk at night
a string of spaced out rags
finger reading the countryside
and avoiding the towns and villages
that signpost our way
staying clear of the drunken militiamen

we have no need to speak
for each is already with the one he loves
hoping that in this most dangerous time
you are safe and not sent away.

Here are my poems Fanni
written in the future on cheap paper
and kept close in the mud of a common grave
where we rest quietly on Hungarian bullets
exhume and read how it was –
as we walk always and forever to Budapest, my love.

Milking-parlour

Now, this is the way a husband keeps his wife
like the closed fingers of a fist
milking the stink of cows in a cold morning barn
by low buzzing electric light
the metal thud of suction pumps

a boy and girl shivering at breakfast
too frightened to speak or make a clumsy move
or come under angry scrutiny

and look how she feels such pain
at having to tie her hair up tight
to hide the grey lank strands
and the office is getting hot now with Spring coming
yet he won't let her fritter money on deodorant
or perfume, or hygiene products –

he says they are an affront to God
but even she knows he does it to control
like the animal rutting late at night
where crying now seems to turn him on
and look at the children, bullied and laughed at

outside school: he simply shrugs
tell your nutty parents to get on with it
and die, leave us the house, the farm
the market garden where he works part time
with the Eastern Europeans, who say among themselves

that he is a pig, but he knows people
and keeps an old service revolver in the loft.
Her father has Alzheimer's and throws small rocks
at the Romanians picking mushrooms
thinking that they are picking his money from the ground
and whispers to his daughter, Things have changed
we live in a foreign country now –
and her mother hisses, You stink down there.

Ohio

Our teachers were threatened
by the unfamiliarly of the sixties and early seventies
heavy set men in tweed jackets
with leather elbow patches
reeking of Woodbines and Mint Imperials

they distrusted the new lads
just out of the universities
with their side-burns and pop art and ban-the-bomb badges
and tight trousers and skinny ties
with their new-fangled teaching methods

why bother? they're only cannon fodder
for the factories and the building sites
and dole queues:

they couldn't stomach what they saw as insolence
the shortened skirts and easy sex
the Che Guevaras and Baader-Meinhofs
had nothing in common with our own "emergency."

This they know, the late night checkpoints
in the sleet, with their sten guns
their duty as B-Specials
the post-war interrogation centres –
the new mind-set of the sixties
was corrupting the youth

Neil Young rising from banned transistors
above the potting and craft sheds
and boys who were fucking at an age
when they had been trapped into dull marriages.

And then the barricades went up
and the nightly riots, the petrol bombs
the soldiers lining the school kids
up on the asphalt yard, in the rain
and trailing out the leaders by their long hair –

Sure, they're only being lads,
defending their own wee country.

Carson's Table

This is not a designated day:
feet echo somewhere on the marble floor of the corridor
a digital phone bleeps in a closed office
dust settles on the picture frames
of dignitaries in bow ties and tails
or frock coats and powdered wigs
on waxen moustaches and full beards

brochures and news sheets hang from racks
bus tours of city trouble-spots
community-centre art festivals
and safe taxis, ethnic self-help groups and forums:

I was a man who believed
in something more than all this
in the destiny and sanctity of every man
in sodomites and barmen and butcher boys
and blood that flows from silver pens –

my grandfather climbs the narrow staircase
to the whitewashed room where all his children sleep
and dresses in this same room
where his heart gave three loud beats and stopped
to cycle thirty miles to the docks
where as an apprentice he watched the men
throw and hammer together bits of rough wood –
all now dead, like the rattle
of rotten sash windows, or a dry religious heart.

As swallows dip and swoop under the city bridges
a ring of lights come on one by one
along the river mouth and the derelict harbours
a siren shrieks on one of the problem housing-estates
Europe sits on the border now like a dark forest
of palisades and barbed wire
America hugs the coast with guns
and emotional lack of understanding

while those who sit in parliament
see Muslims in the woodpile:
a security-guard scared by his own shadow
and myths as black and white as his shoes and shirt
shines a thin torch over the chambers
where Carson's table sits solid and ugly
like a BT cable spool in the dark
and names in blood are always the first
to dry-up, flake, and blow away.

Characters without a Stage

This is almost like a postcard
from somewhere in the past
here, we have burn marks from too great an exposure
the edges browning and crusting over
sadly, obscuring and blurring
the top shutters and veranda of the hotel –
Simferopol springs to mind
but for the frozen ruts of sand and what might be the sea
though it has no colour or form
and could be an indifferent skyline.

To think of Roosevelt, Stalin, and Churchill
playing cards and smoking by lamps
on the top floor is a seductive thought
rounding off figures in millions
forced peasant migrations and displacement
unnatural borders, setting the scenario
for future turbulence –
but after all, a cigar is but a cigar
and at least Stalin is an honest predator
a Siberian snow wolf with Europe in its jaws –

but it's not true, strategists seldom get it right
and anyway, the figures in the foreground
are black and white and modern
mostly poorly dressed or dressed down
in pea-coats and second-hand scarfs and jeans
and are not Tartars, but Dutch beachcombers –
although one I know is Northern Irish –
on a North Sea island.

And the hotel looks exactly as it did over forty years ago
as a recreational hospital-cum-brothel
for shell-shocked Nazi officers
but ask the Irish man about history,
it's fragmented in the blood and psyche.

I remember it was a cold afternoon
one of those December doldrums where nothing had happened
and the sea ebbed and flowed like a hanging life
caught perfectly by her father's old box German camera

and the sea kept coming in, splintering the ice that had formed
as sure as sunlight, or invasions
or cumbersome but certain tanks
with young men like astral babies in leather caps, goggles, earphones
throwing flowers and waves as they eat up the concrete motorways.

Soon this photograph will cease to exist
or at least in another form
like three men rotating an out-of-date map of Europe
in three directions
the anoestrus and mistaken identity of a dark complexioned girl
where vein and flesh atrophied to stone
in a Simferopol mental asylum
strapped on to the bed
to stop her trying to deliver her own imagined child.

SWINE

Rumour has it, among the wide-eyed
and the simply lascivious
that as they approach the place of slaughter
the long functional buildings
grey against a grey sky and tall chimneys,
a great cry goes up
as if from one voice, as if they suddenly realise
why they had been brought there

while all around that morning was so ordinary
the light rain on the cabbage fields
the railway men in blue suits walking to work
the smoking postman on his black bicycle
the hotel workers starting breakfast –
as if they knew, that the fools' journey is really over.

It's hard to keep them placid
you have to cajole them aboard with calm rhetoric
and sometimes it can't be helped –
a slap or a good kick to the arse
and even then, when you have them aboard
the slightest give-away can cause ripples of panic
and upset the whole shebang
regardless, on the approach,
almost as if survival instinct sets in and travels like fire,
they understand.

That morning, as I walked to work
a bright red, gated and slatted lorry,
Hannah's Livestock, Maghera,
came hurtling along the narrow road
the pink dirty arses bulging against the iron
and all at once, with the animal stink and fear,
rose as if one voice, great cries, like children.

At the Movies

Like in a John Wayne movie
my father stepped in out of the blinding sun
all the romantic Hollywood heroes rolled into one
like every soldier disembarking
from the tall sided troopships
duffel bag slung over his shoulder
the fierce desert sun making him look older –
there was nothing he couldn't do

and every time they had a row over housekeeping money
she stopped a while, and saw him once again
giant against the glass ceiling of all that was mundane
and every Sunday, animosity was set aside
as they sat in their armchairs
watching the afternoon matinees
musicals from many years before
singing terrible sounding duos out of tune
or she would come up from the scullery
hands and arms covered in suds
hang over his chair, wet arms around his neck
bawling Forty-Second Street – he looked uncomfortable.

He scooped her up at fifteen on the bridge
where the unemployed men smoked and whistled
a freckled and dreamy girl
for three years he kept up the play act
of pretending never to drink alcohol
until they were married and the top tier of the wedding cake
was lifted by Linfield supporters running past
the café reception, being chased to the station.

As we got older, we thought we understood love
the stand-up fights, and tears, and taking herself off to bed
in the afternoon, her face turned to the wall
from a man who could barely read or write
who couldn't find Cairo on a map
who lost all his teeth when young to pyorrhoea
yet, when he softened, and went sheepishly upstairs
she looked around when the unshaded light came on
and smiled to see how his shoulders filled the chipped doorway.

Queer

And these days the church is all we have left
take the price of bread – how should we live?
no one working, the young marching
the shops shutting down, factories closing
chains and roller shutters and for-sale-signs everywhere,
only the tourists' smile

as they hog the beaches and hotels
only immigrants smile, as they send money orders
back across the sea. Everyone is hurting
even the blow-ins, even the idle whores
undercut by cheap illegals:

he prays morning and evenings at the Catedral de la Anunciacion –
it's his hard earned right – afterwards, he stands
like an old man in a suit on the steps
sometimes, if he can afford it, he makes a trip by bus
out to the fields he sold years before
that are now condominiums for foreigners
and he stands and looks across the sun burnt lawns
and swimming-pools, seeing how it was

now the dust and car fumes of Poligono de Cartuja choke him
at night he can't sleep for horns and sirens and radios
he has no savings left, and his pension
grows less every month to pay the mothers
of black children and heroin addicts

what did we fight for? what did we win?
a young man, strong with the faith
of his country and true church
with his white shirt and black beret and Karabiner 98
he gave the poet and the lame teacher and the two bull-fighters
a cigarette to share – how they trembled
as they took them off the lorry by the side of the road
marched them to the courtyard, to shallow graves
by the rustling olive groves,
one up the arse for the queer.

Summer evenings, he is alone, no one comes to visit
in the yards the smell of hot cooking
and gypsy singing
he watches the ants climb each square of the kitchen tiles
as though they were the stations of the cross:
one true God, but your child who has sang for you
has emptiness in his eyes and a heart without grace.

The Space White

In his madness, my brother saw young girls
hanging round the legs of aunts and uncles
and looking into the house –
they were really there, white and ghostly

who would believe him?
in his world, there were windows behind the clouds
sounds in the morning downpours other than the rain
that only he could hear
his paintings taking him beyond boredom and violence.

The last knife used in Ireland by a father
was drawn across his throat
just breaking the skin
under the Patriarch's hand, like a biblical sacrifice
for daring to walk out with a Catholic girl

who didn't really exist
but who made lewd gestures from behind the wall
of the Parochial House as he walked from school
and covered the badge on his Protestant blazer.

Galloping with the horses on Galway strand
or parading the colours in Portadown
was not an option for an untrained hand

but he saw beyond the wall of mangled furniture
barricading the many divisions
and existed in the only true madness, between the lines.

How I Joined the Communist Party of Ireland

I was thinking of Major Roberts last night
his brown hair sleet as the hair on a Chestnut's back
though he was already in his sixties back then –

or rather, I was thinking of my aunt,
my mother's sister, who looked after me
when my mother worked in the chicken factory
that, like everything else in our small town,
seemed to be owned by Major Roberts' family
and employed most of the local people –

but who kept coming into my thoughts
though he is long dead, like my aunt,
like my mother, with his fast-moving pony and trap
the harness shiny and angry, like his face.

My aunt was a strong woman
with the strength to carry on when her English soldier husband
left her with three kids to look after
as well as myself, setting down values and principles
to live by, rising above poverty
like some Russian in an old book –

and then Major Roberts came galloping
and whipping his pony, the trap hurtling
down the country lane of hawthorn
forcing her into the hedge and pulling me aside
just as the stony faced Roberts flew past
without a look in our direction, without concern
as she betrayed me with the words,
Quick, keep clear for Major Roberts.

The Holding Company

On the bus to the poultry factory –
that is the same one my mother worked in
except it is much bigger now and goes under a Brazilian name
and where two thirds of the workforce are now Eastern European –

I realise, my co-workers are not happy
with their iPhones and their MP3 players
they are not watching the sun burn through the mist
above the wheat fields rolling down to the river.

Watchful communism has been replaced by watchful consumerism:
and The Beast is dead
his body has been exhumed and cremated
his house demolished, airbrushed from history –
and yet you can still buy *Mein Kampf*

and yet you can still watch video clips
of murders and executions from around the world.

People feel powerless, bowing before automated telephone systems
hooked on electrical gadgets
while most of the world starve
while most of the world beat their chests with religious fanaticism
like loud human drums
as three teenagers are shot to death in the Holy Land
thrown into a shallow pit

and more houses are demolished
and a teenager is burned to death in retaliation
and the internet is disconnected for a few angry moments:

when I was a child there was nothing to eat
when I was a child you asked for nothing
you knew not to speak out, no one would listen,
now everyone speaks out, and no one listens

as the bus stops along the carriageway verge
as the East European girls wait already in cars
for shift work customers
as Ireland becomes another subway stop
in the decline of Western culture
as we disappear beyond the bicycle sheds
the narrow corridor to the killing rooms.

Part 3

Pathways

When You Are Old

I want to be an old man without worries
I don't want to grow into a battered armchair
in a one bedroom, damp council flat
on a dry angry estate
where the police are indifferent, or afraid to go
and everyone pays homage to the local hood commander

and everything reeks of pee and mould
old clothes tattered and not what you would choose to wear
a side rack of tablets
for heart failure or cancer or depression

and a fat bitch who hates men
gives you food you can't eat
throws out your books touched with mildew
puts you to bed at five o'clock
where you lie on your back staring at a cracked ceiling

listening to children out in the yards
hoping no one will smash your door in
trying not to think of the dripping toilet that makes you want to go
and wondering why your body is tired, has packed up
how you don't recognise the deterioration of your soul.

Days are spent, grey on grey,
looking out at a never changing street
the poetry books on the broken shelf are a constant reminder
of what you once tried to say

letters come from faraway places,
Can I have permission? Are you still alive?
but you don't answer your tormenters
like the splintered tree outside the flat
that died before it was truly dead.

The Examination Board

My mother would take us one by one by the hand
to the welfare office, the speech therapist, the private doctor
whose practice was on the tree lined street of posh houses –

it felt strange, in a freaky way, while the estate was quiet
the others at school, you felt special, for a while,
and then the play stopped, and you wondered what was different about you
and the neighbours were talking over you

and wasn't it odd, when we turned in to the street
the workmen repairing bomb-damaged drains
my father scowling from the lorry-cab window
slugging from lemonade bottles of baking soda and water,
wasn't it strange, that my mother knew not to approach him
or wave, or make eye contact, while he was it work
and even stranger, I knew it, could sense the oddness in him

the child's mind is rich in detail
the child's mind is vague in what it strives to forget:
there were posters of dogs and English children on the cream coloured walls
and the man smelled of pipe tobacco and talked mostly to my mother
I think I cried and kicked over a table – but was it true?

being Protestant, we had no one in Brooklyn or Boston to send us parcels
being Protestant, we were too proud
but pride didn't put food in the cupboard, or stop the humiliation
from petty Government officials, or rent agents –
and then it stopped, and even now I can't decide,
was I a freak or a genius, or the cat cradle of ignorance.

The wide blue yonder

Sometimes, in a moment, the mind gets a rush
like a train entering and leaving a short tunnel
like the first time I saw a bomb going off

the excruciating silence, then the strange barking of dogs
before the pavement began to tremble under your feet
and the buildings shuddered, followed by a deafening bang
the crazy sound of sirens, walls imploding, screams
dust billowing out like sea clouds
the million flapping shredded office blinds –

and I didn't realise until much later
that I was bleeding, streaming down my face
it all seemed so impersonal
that I never thought of blaming anyone

or like the rush of speed in a girlfriend's flat in Amsterdam
that left me sick and seeing not beauty but the ugliness of things
of how man can corrupt what is natural in life
of how a girl's face can seem ravaged with death –

and then I looked beyond the level of the Belfast street
to the God carved mountains, and listened to each blade of grass
as it grew towards the sun, and was filled with the understanding,
that eternity is only a second.

The May King

I was the best dressed girl in our estate
slacks with foot straps
fancy brogues with fan shaped tongues
skinny roll tops
public-school girl's green tracksuit

hand-me-downs from a well-off cousin –
I rode out across the estate on my paper-round
oblivious to the sniggers, the shouts, the insults
from other school-kids, and adults alike
as I waited outside the local bookies
to place my father's racing bets

losing the affection of the only girl
who had ever shown an interest –
she couldn't handle the embarrassment

and I learned quickly how to fight
the street way, reducing other boys to tears by my viciousness
sometimes, guiltily, without provocation.

This is what poverty is, a set of circumstances
beyond your control, enforced from inside the circle
by a father too lowly paid to care about cruelty
by a mother too stretched to listen –
I understood early, how we all bend.

Around Christmas time, when the snow was on the greens
the travelling woman and her kids
would come round all the doors
selling wooden clothes-pegs
that you could buy in the street market for half the price –

I patted my pockets to show I had nothing
and she sneered and cursed a century's old curse
under her alcohol breath –
the first time I felt ashamed.

The Child

My mother was the child I conceived
standing at the window on 42nd street
waiting for her to come home from the factory
with the songs from the matinee musicals
she sang as a young girl

a freckled, brown haired Elizabeth Taylor
with a defective terrier
that had its last fit
in her father's bucket of cold water

while she hid in the bearded long grass
on Bluebell Hill
among the ghostly barns and banging doors
that held no more terror.

And I always felt that it was I
who took her by the hand
and explained the physical world
my father clumped through in his clumsy work boots.

Now that they are all dead
she has no home to return to –
the second-hand clothes are piled together
like the garments of the executed

the paste jewellery rubbing white
the army pocket book archaic:
I watch her running, laughing under the railway bridge
sticking haws to the jumpers
of her brothers and sisters

and die again before her image
so that she might live
in this world a little longer.

Letter from the Republic of London

It's been a long time since I've paid a visit, or written –
my writing was never good, and with my Liam's death
I thought things would get better
but I'm more lonely now than when we first came over
and nobody knows anyone's name round here
(if you could pronounce it)

yesterday, the neighbour from the next door flat
who never speaks, who has scars on her face
stole the yard-brush I keep outside
where I always leave it to sweep the landing –
that upset me for some reason

and the bars here are full of Irish people
I don't know, they seem cemented to the sixties
you need to have eyes like a fly round here
once, these Muslim men cursed at me for smoking
outside on the street, knocked the cigarette from my mouth
at night you treble-bar the door
and become gaga in front of the telly.

I would ask you to visit, but I don't think you'd like it
maybe when the Hammers are at home
but every work-day I disappear into the city
like all the bloodless faces going down
the steps to the subway, and I clean offices
and pretend to be deaf rather than offend

when I come back again, I listen to the neighbours fighting
in tongues. The buildings here are Shards and Gherkins
and Smoothing Irons of metal and glass
and long trains that curve through the houses
below my flat, but even twenty storeys up
the planes and the blue open sky seem such a long way off.

Two Blue Moons

My father lies below the green medicated water
a menacing shadow beneath a flat stone –
there is no shame here, a slash of pubic hair
laid bare for all to see, and ignore
but for the ripples beneath the mind
and the too-bright light bulbs
screwed into the high ceiling

the chipped and flaking enamel bath
the terror as the tepid water laps the chin –
they are trying to do me in – and I feel him
against my skin, but say nothing
for any protest is seen as dissent
the spiral strips of the medulla unravelling
like the speed of light – it pays to be sly

and swallow the unpalatable, the living food
that moves slowly across the plate
the sudden appearance of the living dead
in the corner of the room at T.V. recreation time
and remember when painting with fingers
as the man in the suit asks mockingly kind,

What is it? to reply, Can't you see?
become immune to all reactions
for reality is unsure of itself
the old men in tears who wank without ejaculation
the woman who comes into your room
and hurts you as you sleep
dry as a leaf chafed by fingers
like nightmares that awake from the blue deep

my father speaks with a loud voice
among the tables and the dying flowers
he tells me those from outside are already dead
like electrical leads and sockets and broken glass
and sit around the wrong bed
a chorus line of devious nodding fools.

Some days the fog around the shrubberies clear –
there was a gate leading to a bottom field
and washing flapping on a Spring line like angry birds
a kitchen steamed with the loss of light
but then the reverse becomes true
two moons blue in the evening sky
and a husband ten feet tall screaming strange commands
trying to make me believe I was born mother and child.

September brings a false rain dead
against the double window panes
news carries like a distant scream
and can't be true in this snow-shaker world
while regurgitated food is passed around with sniggers
while hand on shoulder we shuffle on slippered feet
round the kaaba of our waking dreams
and my father raises himself on a bony elbow and winks
having seen it all so many times before.

Remember

The moon is round and bright this early morning
like the face of a child who couldn't cry
but beat her head with perfect rhythm
against the iron bars of an orphanage bed

and died, sitting upright, a Buddha before flaking paint
frozen like the frozen lights
suspended in the windows of the council estate.

The dogs sniffing each other on the greens
seem to know so much more than us –
and it is deathly silent
like before snow, or hoar frost crackling on the pavements

each in his own oblong box before the morning brings redemption
cars on carriageways passing each nondescript town
down the line, knots in a rope:

when I was an orphan, they shaved our heads
to stop the lice finding beds of dirty thick-headed hair
body functions of the young were paramount
to virtues of health or sin or temptation

the arranged fights with older boys in the stone yard
you couldn't win
the bloody beltings for torn clothes.

My sister shines in this shiny new world
her round face blistered with craters of neglect –
the day they lifted her into the ground
they locked us in to settle us down

but everything orbits to its own still end
as people pass, others come in
and change the wallpaper, the second-hand beds, the law
and keeps the hunger just that little bit above

like dull lights popping out one by one
like blues and reds and yellow flares of carriageways
fading into mountainous daylight.

The Blow Fly

These are the dimming years of my life
between the balmy summer evening and dusk
a life well spent, if over-short,
among the bulrushes and orchids and pond lilies
of this tangled woodland copse

this is my world, don't ask me how I got here
or how I came to be, far from the mechanical sounds
of that other world seen askew
that shimmers beyond the wire and the long grass –

I ventured there once, when younger
and I had the strength
but the air was heavy and sweet and over-crowded –
those were the glory days, king of the corpses
working hard among the funeral pyres
the glowing heat of the chimney bricks
the belching ovens, the open sores

too much of a good thing, you drown
and grow fat and sluggish with abundance
so I drifted up and away, resting on the white sheets
of the fraulein's washing, and missed the quiet spaces
the clear sunlight, cow-pats, and the wild meadow flowers.

The First Day of Creation

The first to arrive, were the guys with the generator
and then there was no noise at all
but the biting wind pulling and shaking
the rubber tipped window frames
and the squirrels nesting under the lino-covered floorboards.

The lights are popping on one by one
in the rooms across the road
the chamber maids from Eastern Europe
are changing the bed sheets –
in the synthetic light, they look forlorn
and a hundred years old.

A little later, someone will appear
at the corrugated pulley-operated door
for a quick smoke, but is blown back in again
and the sound of lorries unloading clatter
metallic and foreign along the road.

And then there is light, just slightly
breaking the dark in the East
above the river and the fields
like a religious painting
though there is nothing numinous in this scene.

And my thoughts become bare trees and wind damage
the lonely braying of a lost animal:
what gave birth to me was never human
lies not far from here
and rots in the ground
the organs that nourished me, are gone
the brain that conceived me, is lost
so that I came only from a rack of bones –

and the East European girl looks at the morning
a moment from the window
before sighing, and is far away
as the room light fades into the light of day.

John L. Burns

They say it started with shoes –
but shoes were important back then
the state of your feet could be the end of you:

John L. Burns sits out on the rocker
in front of his shack
he is seventy, but his eyes have seen more
tired of looking on bodies
that have been pounded into the rich earth
like rotting vegetables
or lying like children's snow angels
along the ditches, flies open
and faces frozen in shock.

He didn't know if he wanted his picture taken at first
but when they came and set-up the camera
he relented, so he looks kind of proud
if a little apprehensive
unsure of what a hero is supposed to look like

his musket at a ready angle against the pockmarked wall
crutches behind him, in his semmit, torn trousers, and socks
his hands folded like a missionary

and the whitewashed walls, splintered door
the window broken and stuffed with rags
building rubble heaped on one side
the collapsed porch propped up with broken brick and wood poles –

it could be a house on the Ballymoney Road
the same stubborn squalor and outside privy:
my uncle could be John L. Burns –
he threw a stick for Tullygarley –
his lean angular jaws set tight with pride and fear
the clear blue eyes of religious intent.

What does a hero do when time moves on?
John L. Burns sits in his rocker
looking out across the fields of wheat
and muses on the vast scope of small things
my uncle in hobnails that were far too big for him
pulled by his mother from the ranks of the Local Defence Volunteers

cried like a sickly child –
John L. Burns resettles his broken feet
sees the dome of the White House rising above the fields
and smiles – of this defiance in the face of futility,
nations are made.

On Watching Men Cut Down a Tree

It's like a Chinese puzzle
working backwards from natural growth
the cherry picker bobbing up and down
one man holding a heavy branch
while the other lops it off with a buzzing chainsaw

like dismantling an old mill brick by brick
or tracing back the bloodline branches of a cancer
or other malignant disease to its origin
until there is nothing left to work on
but the stumped trunk that with no more to prune
and is dug out

gone, was never grown from a seed
branching up to the light
nourished by rain and sun
majestic and indifferent to the fumbling lovers
from the hotel disco, the upcountry coach trips

twigs fed into wood shredders
sawdust and resin brushed and shovelled into bags
the crack and flare of burning sticks –
where once there were wooden houses, sweat-shops, temples
people, gentle winds – there is nothing.

Star Man

The early morning hours are the quietest
someone might come off a shift
someone's routine world might be overturned
by an event they couldn't control
at an hour they had no say in
the foreign lights of the hospital
that disorientate as they suck you in.

Sometimes an animal will nose about
in the rubbish bins and knock about tins
or a woman will hurry along from a one night stand
bereft of emotion now, different in tight clothes
and sordid make-up from the night before
head full of promises
and afraid of her own echo in heels.

Then the morning grows light
with the first yawning bicycle
a car or van will stop, but turn
realising their mistake, you sit back down
and think of the time you had nothing but time
when all you wanted was to be touched

and soon you realise that you are held in this place
like a child's spinning-top
and for that moment you are as bright and clear
as the North Star, or the light in the window
of the house with the stone garden
farther down the road, before it fades
in a woman's morning sleep.

A Pair of Praying Hands

The world is stained yellow and smells of tobacco
such is the innocence of childhood
that these same fingers that prod and probe
were intimate with my mother
and maybe other women as well
who maybe smiled and reset my hair

the knuckles busted open in a bar fight
the nails flattened with a paving slab
the swirls of time and wear and spittle-cleansing
and digging along the line in hard weather
huddled in the pockets of a second-hand ulster

aligned like a hair trigger
a brilliantined finger aimed at some mother's son
with whom he had a derry
that whetted a bayonet like the fine cut of a playing card.

These hands, formed within a womb
were no bigger than a thumbnail
learned quickly to grab and reject
before they took me by the hair
and locked me in a room without light or water
one finger shortened by a falling crankshaft
that made flesh and blood and bone of iron

wind and rain and frost and age
grew liver spots upon closed fists
and raised me up like a fingerprint
to be unique in another story
and handed down the folded palms
to nail and wood and earth and resignation.

Inside Out

My father dragged all our furniture onto the green
the settee, chairs, and carpets looked forlorn
ridiculous in the summer dusk. He switched on the lamps
and made things less obscure by marking out perimeters
that kept to the measurements of our livingroom.

He sits heavily in his favourite chair
defiant, in his stockinged feet,
he opens another beer and lights-up
people and dogs walk past and stare
as if looking through windows
children sit on bicycles, rocking in stunned silence.

My sister curls her washed hair and watches
the clock without a mantelpiece
for her Catholic boyfriend who keeps
to the other side of the imaginary but very real line
she goes to the invisible door to meet him
and drive around the estate in a stolen at least dodgy car.

Stay away from the windows, what windows?
my mother tells my older brother with cropped hair,
In case they see that you are home on leave –

then she goes to the kitchen to wash-up dishes
a migraine predicting the coming weather
my father opens another beer and turns on the boxing
it is getting dark, people drift away bored
as I count the lights popping-on along the carriageway
and wait for the promised rain.

Mapland

I am no Imran Khan
I never played the English game
I never had any power
I never found beliefs

my lovers teeth rotted away
and never were replaced
her eyes are always happy
she talks like Janis Joplin
she is no model
she has no modesty
she takes power in its lowest form

and takes sad pictures of her twelve-year old son
in a too big school uniform
in each one he tries to smile through terror
picked upon
his geography places countries
in absurd physical relationships –
oceans like ice-caps like deserts
don't exist –
maybe the earth is flat after all

and no bigger that the boarded-up houses
of this Northern estate:
England is no bitch
she has football and game shows and tolerance
and is closer than an obscure language
or a second cousin
yet different enough to blame

for welfare cuts and baton rounds
and lost sports togs and broken pencils
and the girls who laugh at his sewed-up trousers

the Himalayas are a made-up place
in a film called Shangri-La
the Punjab and Peshawar are types of curry
from the Hot & Spicy Takeaway
Bid Laden is the president of America (or is it the USA?)

my lover and her son are not dumb
she relishes ignorance as she collects
the common colloquialisms
and sometimes she is profoundly right
in matters of sexuality or abuse
and sometimes I am twelve
and sometimes I am the purple mountain ridges

cutting across the fat of her belly
like Imran Khan looking up doe-eyed
from her woman's magazine
or her son cutting strange ciphers
into his thin arms after school.

Huguenot

He could never be one of us
everything about him was different
even his English was not our English

his clothes fitted without stitching
or turn-ups or patches
he was clean to the point of distraction,
almost shiny
although his skin was darker

he was wrong on so many counts
and ripe for it –
the teachers exalted him
but no one got too close

someone said his father sketched birds
for a nature magazine
yet it seemed more plausible
that he came over to see the installation of machinery
for the new tyre factory

and someone said, My father said
they only employ Catholics there.

The first time we set upon him
we lured him to the corner of the high red brick wall
where we played handball
and kicked his legs from under him
into the overflowing drain –
we searched for a crucifix
how were we to know there were Protestants in France.

After that, he kept to himself
under the window of the headmaster's office –
and then he was gone, as sudden as school days
as sudden as ignorance
having left a chalked message on the blackboard,
Fuck your Queen and your King Willie.

Part 4

Mile Stones

How I Discovered Livingstone

I found Livingstone in the stone Sunday-school
on Casement Street, among the fag butts
the chewing-gum, leg scabs, bone white breasts.

Livingstone, Livingstone – that's a stone town in Scotland
with a big waterwheel:
my Sunday-school teacher came from there
before he left the better half of his brain
at Narrow Water.

I met Livingstone on the Tanganyika shoreline
a large man gone to seed –
that was after I changed my name

on the sluggish yellow backwater
behind the gas-works and St. Pat's boxing-school
they showered me with glass, bedsprings, rocks,
clumps of dried cow dung –

What happened to Livingstone? I asked my father,
His arse dropped out like a baboon's!

I was never missing, Livingstone said
a name in my Sunday-school prize-giving book
as my father sent me up for bread and a good hiding,
You'll find me up on the headwaters, all alone in my whiteness
searching thirty years for a God in my own wilderness

and seeing only perplexed faces looking at me
talking in tongues in a hell of my own making:

Not true, I answer, you were always sure of your way
in that dark continent of the soul,
the darkening after-class of a sinner reading
the red map, the slave routes, the rainy season on a slate roof.

The Zoo

The horror was in their enjoyment of our ignorance:
my father spoke with a broken tongue, and passed it on
the wonderment of bananas in a wooden crate
a little grinning man in a wide hat who made us smile
children from a council estate caught up in the Markets

the Victorian hall of wrought iron:
You couldn't put them into new houses, they'd piss in the sinks
have never seen an inside toilet before –
shrivelled heads on the posts of a picket fence
round a Meeting House, or in Africa, or in Ecuador
or bobbing down the road after an explosion.

Ecuador, Ecuador, I'd repeat to myself, having seen it on some sticker
seeing wide palm leaves and banana trees and rubber vines
while not really knowing the distance between oceans
or in the mind: teach us to speak properly, oh father
like a white man with manicured nails
or a civil servant in the Housing Trust
or a Presbyterian minister looking for somewhere to sit
in our cluttered front room, before prayer

I saw men with crossed bandoleers, somewhere on the border
outside Silver Bridge where my father delivered concrete heads,
blood dull machetes, coca sniffing Indians
who could trail you through jungles for miles at a run,
and the revolution: when they cut off hands and feet
of Congo children, it was the hands and feet
of all us poor children, who would find voices

and ask out of want, for the blank spaces on a map
for fit-to-live-in new houses, to have the same as you
to know where bananas come from –
Belfast docks. Liverpool, mister –
sitting under Queen Victoria's skirts, like all good unwashed heathens
the warped mind, like the Congo pygmy in a Brussels zoo
sharing his space with a hippopotamus.

Bach

The nightshift has just finished
mops buckets dusters buffer
are put back in the cupboards –
everyone is tired, everyone is yawning
the first cars on the Arnhem bridge
look lonely and foreign
who is making strong coffee?
time for a burn down in the cells
just make sure you keep the heavy door open
the photographs on the office tables –
notes from the house of the dead –
are coming into focus again
I wonder if she is sleeping alone?
dirty glasses and broken capsules on the cabinet
roaches flattened between the pages of my literature books
Paul flings open the fire-door
and a rush of morning air and rain
assails the lungs – he slept with her last week
and keeps apologising, the asshole
sit down to just-made toast
how can they stomach sprinkling the bread
with sugar beads, beads of chocolate?
Was Dostoevsky shot by firing-squad?
No, he was an epileptic! Dutch humour, everyone laughs,
Turn on the radio, tune into Bach,
and the old women shake their heads –
especially Het with her faded registration number
tattooed on a thin blue arm –
at the students who know books and music
but nothing about real life
or the miracle of fresh baked bread.

Narcissus

All the shades are drawn along Alt-Marzahn
the early evening sun boils like blood in the brain
with the smell of onions, garlic, peppers, curry
the rattling of apartment doors
the hiss of radios
the clatter of feet on bare stairs
and children's games –

I think I have no need to worry
I think I am that parrot in its cage on the windowsill
locked inside here like a case-study
in a nineteenth century German/Jewish study
of scuffed furniture, freeze-dried flowers, bottled foetuses –
surely things change, the world now moves to a different neurosis.

You don't work, she tells me, as a tram hits the electric link
outside at the terminus, but I want her to leave
in my silence, so that I can work on this poem
so that I can curl in the embryonic fluid of my book
on deviants: why should I care
about wilted vegetables from the second-hand market
sold from the boot of the Turkish man's car

soil heavy and discoloured on the draining board
in the small kitchen
where she douches between her legs
so as not to have to visit the communal toilet
with its rats and porno pictures
and the ghosts of history
and the ghosts of the displaced.

I worked last week, at any costs
loading lorries with bags of cement for the new Germany
and felt like a real workman
as valid as the prostitute on the floor above
who energetically fucks the afternoons away
with heavy-set salesmen from the Middle East
and who calls me Ba-be when we meet on the landing
just like regular neighbours:

oh where are you Freud, we need you again –
I am afraid of horses, penises, and pubic hair –
passing judgement on the things we never knew
about ourselves, the sexual violence, the kink,
the honour killings, stonings, beheadings,
the burning of mosques, synagogues, sex-cinemas,
and a poet who believes he is the reincarnation of himself
from better and more prophetic times.

Sibyl

My sister worked Saturdays and afternoons in Kingsland
a stern girl who flowered in the late sixties
she never smiled
hair bowl-cut round freckles
and eyes that said, I'm no adolescent fool

trays of cheap rings, plastic bangles,
ponytail bobs, Tupperware, Taiwan toys
pick'n'mix sweets
Hunters and Coopers parked outside on the street
wondering if any moment they might explode into little pieces
the same grid of closed-over scars

why was she so angry?
thumping the keys of the heavy till
smoking stolen cigarettes in the stockroom
courting squaddies with her fat mate in the forest
and drinking bottles of Silver Crown

glum-faced with the crippled boy
in a wet Trafalgar Square, taking pictures –
even the bedraggled pigeons wanted to fly away –
and Carnaby Street wasn't the bohemia she thought it would be:
her fat friend worked down the street from her
pounding the wooden boards of Woolworths
until she was trapped by the barred windows
at the back of the store
burned to death by incendiaries –

after the funeral, my sister helped to lock
and bar her own workplace in protest.
On the last day of school, frumpy in her hand-stitched dress
at the townhall fleadh, among the grammar school girls,
reading from Little Gidden – she didn't understand a word of it –
and when she came home in silence
she threw her plate of food at the wall and screamed
into the face of the coming years.

Fishing Upper Silesia

There were no beautiful Loughs or blue flag beaches
oil seeped into puddles and storm drains
brown builder's sand from the back of my father's lorry
studded with half bricks
was useless for making castles:

look at your black hair, little eel
the sad face of a sickly child
at your first communion

the Polish priest is certain, Winds are imminent
God has given up the world for one hundred years –
ship-yard cranes are silent

rows of faces, like miners' daughters
no one smiles
silent, eyeless fishes.

My mother's first marriage home
was a damp council flat:
she sat on the only chair, afraid to swim
through the room's echo
afraid of the old woman's brush-shaft
banging on the ceiling

only her breath, only her breathing
until my father came back from work.

And as God took in his children
my friend refused to give
to a collection for political prisoners
was beaten comatose with bricks and pick-axe handles –

he rarely speaks, but now the Iron Curtain is down
and Polish girls chatter with local accents
he goes fishing every year to Upper Silesia –
he thinks no one knows Upper Silesia –

and sits immovable like a blood clot
or a passing cloud over chemical puddles
as the tall belching chimneys inside an endless blue sky
like a frozen woman in a cold room
like a small trout in a white dress.

Kite

Our science teacher was obsessed with aerodynamics
ornithology flight
quantum physics of parallel histories
spitfires over Germany

and a selection of smutty postcards
of Berlin prostitutes he bought in the war
we stole from his desk drawer
and made clumsy planes out of:

my father fought in the war –
mostly tedium
Palestine dust and flies and whores.

The only thing he ever made me was a kite
two crossed pieces of cheap dowel rods
brown wrapping paper
a long tail of cord and twisted newspaper

a Chinese man
a head in a basket hanging from a telegraph-wire:
Benjamin Franklin was a presenter in Play School.

In quantum tests, perhaps my father's kite
flies above the factory cooling towers
the hill where traitors were hung drawn and quartered
entrails left like raw linen to bleach in the sun
gleaned bones of wax –

but here on this plane my father's kite
never left the ground
of broken glass, old bed springs, rusty tin, greyhound shit
entangled in barbed wire.

When I brought it home to him
he smashed it and threw it on the fire –
such is physics

my science teacher's wooden limb
trapped in a single gauge line
he found out, he was not aerodynamic, only rail ballast.

The Running Man

Spain is cruel
she watches me behind the luggage lockers
of the local train stations

it is the power of the sun
and the far-off line between sky and scorched earth
that makes mulch out of steel
streaked meat out of mucus

fabricated metal twist like paper –
ask Lorca
ask Goya
or the peasant dark as skin
or the Indian green as maize
or the line of students face down in a shallow ditch.

When the rain comes it is like bullets
from machine-guns
peppering the dry ground
walls to mud
fields to mud
dreams to mud.

This woman sleeps behind flaking shutters
this woman sleeps with every man
she is a small boat from Morocco
the priests are afraid of her

the Olympic pool is diseased water
the ferry leaves for the Islas Baleares
in a Miro painting of water and light.

In Ulster we spoke of Spain
the way we spoke of executions
like a green Madrid stamp
before the package holidays
made everything crass and normal

the old men fat and naked
holding hands on the beach
or like the children stoning salamanders
in the heat of the tongue-dry river beds.

The Piano Player

Don't ask me, I'm only the driver
my mini skirt pulled high at the checkpoints
my wristwatch set at three
the dials on the dashboard, points of light:

I am on the edge of a forest at night
a grey fringe of moor-land
the jagged rooftops and aerials
of large housing-estates under a ragged sky
of failing luminance, of crows roosting

like fields climbing deeper up the mountainsides
to a spreading darkness,
and the little girls at the street-ends
folding-up their skipping ropes
why, I even stopped outside Dundalk
to buy fish and chips and cigarettes:

stupid ignorant woman like a cracked jug
on a window-sill, dirty fingernails
a pile of piss-stinking nappies

a simple soul on the back seat
skinny bony thing that could slip under
too shell-shocked in the coming headlights
to realise the great and terrible future
that we are speeding into –
don't blame me, I'm only the driver.

Path

The dog in the street knows who you are
lowest of the low
banging into Americans
flea-coat for St-Lazare

up here in the high-risers
Billy clubs, graffiti, freight trains
concrete cafes
teeth-sucking sugared tea
bog-holes without lights
shit-print walls

have you some work for me?
a parcel to deliver from my unclean hands?
down to the hair-stylists on the Magenta
among the lazy markets and wasted veins.

Mo-Mo lives in an automatic toilet on St-Germain
his madness keeps the whores away
dripping water
blood stained toilet sheets
syringes, floating condoms
but he loves the buzz
the cross-city green prison vans
the Canadian cameras –
he loves to fuck white boys.

I crossed the border with a young German girl
too young to be travelling with
two North Africans lured her from me in Narbonne
by playing to her hunger
by bread and a train ticket back to Berlin.

In this Medina, far from the heart
the girls in flowing robes and veils are like swans
gliding across the square of stunted Plane trees
and bird-shit swings, like swans, like white swans
as an airliner climbs clumsily into the sky
for somewhere that is not the West
far from sirens, tree huggers, begging bowls
the cardboard boxes of ink cartridges and sport's clothes:

and when he looked out across the desert
he could see his followers navigating
sometimes hidden water holes
by the steadfast blindness of their faith
even though the sand dunes
blew away and shifted in the hot winds.

Shlomo

Little Greek boy listening to the radio
through the open door of the taxi –
there are only two radios in Salonika
both in taxis –

all of Europe is talking
all of Europe is ranting
all of Europe is barking mad
all of Europe cries for bread.

My mother is born in a carpenter's house
the walls are whitewashed like Greek islands
a tall man could reach out
and touch wall to wall with his fingertips
stretch out and touch the outside toilet
with his shiny boots.

A barrel of cooking-oil
from the warehouses at the docks –
they are carrying away everything
before the Italians arrive.

Salonika, Salonika, Swastika,
pelvic bones are the hardest to grind down:
my father was the same age
barefoot in the spinning mills
he lost his toenails from standing long hours
in fetid water

as my mother choked in wood dust
and the radios talked of war
and the cattle trucks had barbed-wire windows

and an eagle appears high above the blue waters
the bare rock cliffs
circles high in the sun above its prey –
then is suddenly gone.

Kafka's Travelling Corpse

When I think of The Castle
I see Bruegel's hunters in the snow
long androgynous figures in crew necks
devoid of feeling anything other than bare existence
weighed down by the usefulness
of their shoddy caps and shoes

we don't see the threadbare
the head lice, the unwashed sexual organs

somewhere there must be an inn burning wood
and rooms where red hands
wring garments and serve beer
perhaps a small room in a bell-tower
girls with physical defects having sex with unwilling men.

When I think of The Castle
I see the landscapes of Jean Paul Lemieux
where nothing much happens in the whiteness of the canvas
where everything explodes in the heaviness of black slanted lines

like the angular Jewish/German lines in Kafka's face
the sharpness of Doberman ears:

on the street where my aunt lived
false archways over doors led to shadowed nothingness
telephones were black and heavy and unused
squatting like giant beetles

chickens ran in the courtyard pecking beetles
meter-men stole feathered eggs
the crazy woman in the next yard
had caked excrement on her hands and clothes –
they would have zapped her

like a million Kafkas
like you Kafka
in your suit and stud collar
your corpse travelling coalscuttle-like into a clear Prague sky.

Don Quixote and Sancho Panza

This tall ship has many creaking floors
among its riggings, where little light
comes through, and the wind
sways the top masting
with its narrow opaque windows:

or it could be a giant windmill
the hypnotic slow wafting of its sails
the crankshafts, and chutes
rotating, wringing the last moisture
from the tired and dried-up planks:

and the teacher warns, Don't smoke,
the dust particles in the air
will catch fire and explode
and kill all of us – there are slower ways to die

look at these men, small and squat
slow under cwt bags of meal
like coal miners, like salt mine workers
round and round, through hatches
like Dante's first circle
like rolling boulders up a steep hill:

a great mechanical doll
that vibrates and shudders
with heavy machinery, down to its foundations –

in such places, my family sweated
in such places, we would too
there is no place for a working-class poet who was born here
a gaggle of boys laughing into the years ahead
only the moment, like the two whippet dogs
fucking in the alley between the flour mill and the police station.

Five Points

I dream borders, red map lines
running through frozen pine forests
snow peaked mountain ranges
black Bogland, dilapidated hill farms cut in two
mail trains carrying diseases along veins
and broken lungs as we sleep.

My father could wallow in the distance beneath his eyes
fight a war without understanding the morality
could never find the deserts he fought in on any map –
he found me a large atlas in a rubbish skip
hard blue cloth covers
psychical features of unknown lands
in brown, green, and blue contours

even then, I knew things had changed
that borders had been pushed aside by suffering
the sun had set on Manchuria
the Tsar's brains made mosaics on a wall in Ekiterinburg
Musil died while exercising and the Franz List
steamed and rolled from Budapest to Vienna
Ireland deep as a berry like a quarter of the world:

still, I could dream, a puppeteer residing above people
who were there, yet were no longer there
I could still see burning villages, men on horseback –

where are you now my mother?
lost in uncharted lands
a girl again, who thought the border
was a real presence, a dry stone wall, a ditch.

My father climbed over his own death in cruel pain
my aunt lay back into her's with a gasp
but my mother became a child again
walking miles into the clicking of a respirator.

And I dream a nightmare country
a station beneath pointless far-off stars
where migrants wait on wooden benches in waiting-rooms
and khaki soldiers sleep along the track humped like dead whales

and my mother is young again
a young woman without human boundaries
who has found love in a strange place.

The Rising Sun

So many dead bodies on this Pacific rock
like silver sardines picked up in a wind tunnel
and left neatly in rows on this thin lipped beach
only the oscillation of limbs and hair in the waves
like the wind blowing in the broad leafed palms –

I wished I had died, my uncle cried in his hospital bed,
all those years ago, what a waste
and the cruelty that came afterwards

like the hot sun higher on the rock
the beatings with whips and iron bars

blood flows easily in the sun
everything rots and stinks and never heals over
and the bodies rolling over in the waves
as if turning on to their sides to sleep.

He could never forgive
not even the coolies or forced-labour natives
who stood around grinning at every execution
the young bearded Australian, blindfolded and bound
kneeling over a shallow grave he was made to dig

the sun blindingly reflecting on the Japanese officer's
round glasses and shin gunto sword
that sliced the head off in one stroke
the blood spurting from the still kneeling body

to the cheers of joy and laughter
and the young Japanese officer strutted away
with his hard-on visible in his pants:

I wish I had died too, but I was a young man
and a coward, and ate insects in the dirt
and called them master, and cried when they beat me –
I wanted to live a few minutes more

then he died: only our deaths are certain
as we left him on the white sea of the hospital bed
and that afternoon, there was a sudden storm
that littered the beach and rocks with floundering dying fish.

Bukowski

To be a good lover, you have to be on welfare,
Bukowski said that, as he strode across the bar
of the Santa Monica racetrack
with his beard and his whiskey and water
and the biggest balls in the world –

but I guess your woman has to be ugly too
and wine crazy, and not too clean
cooking pancakes on a dry pan
haemorrhaging on flophouse beds:

what would Bukowski say about my friend
spreading newspaper in the garden shed to crap on
neutered by his wife's spick and span bathrooms
taking his shoes off at the back door?

or my lover, a habitual drunk
who dirtied herself in a French commune
and stunk all day like the garbage pails –
I helped to clean her up, now that is love too.

Punch her in the mouth, Bukowski told me,
go out and take a drink, then get it down
before you sober – I got the first train out,
I was a coward too

and fell in love with the old Japanese woman on Waikiki beach
the skin blistering from her thighs and legs
her hair matted like the sea waves
everything she owned folded into a canvas bag
a rake for raking stones and twigs –
she barked like a dog every time I passed her:
Bukowski eats dog.

My friend is on Prozac, my lover is on the game
Robert Louis sits under the hau trees
and Bukowski looks for his wallet in a hangover crap
down the bog at Santa Monica –
his books have outgrown us both.

The game's up kid, ask Cupcake –
senile old man, writing poems about cats
crying at his wedding ceremony
bleeding through his skin, like an old lover
or a drunk who couldn't box but could tell the truth.

Concrete Cows

Astronauts can't cry in space
like concrete cows
they float on fields of someone else's dreams:

Yuri Gagarin went farther
into the embryonic darkness –
it took him one-hundred and eight minutes to circle himself

before he crashed seven years later
into the earth
like concrete cows kicked over onto their sides
one by one

and people marched in silence through the bleak hills
that Yuri couldn't see from space
as my father watched Cassius Clay
and wondered where the white men had gone

and I envied my well-off school-friend
who had a Spiderman bed-spread
whose father packed-up his family
took a job at Aldermaston in the brave sixties.

Every night my father fought with the television
a world gone mad
everything was only studio made anyway

as we made space modules
from liquid soap bottles and egg cartons
with American flags stuck on the noses

put together poppies or sprigs of shamrock
as people looked over mountains
and were beaten senseless with iron bars
with pickaxe-handles

my father cursing at the telly –
for a moment Gagarin forgot he was Russian
as he looked down upon the blue earth
while concrete cows began to dream
and my father couldn't understand why he beat me nightly.

Xenophanes in Hell

Everything was simpler then, or so it seemed
underneath the rafters of our rented room
somewhere there were broad rivers and boats
before the screams, and on the wooden panelled walls
were pictures of Brahma, sunflowers, de Beauvoir
and bottles stood like old lovers along the shelves.

Xenophanes knows there is one God
if a dog could draw, he would draw God in his own image:
I know that dreams are real
I know that the dead who come to her are real
like the photographs of young men on grave stones
like disfigured lepers in an Indian hostel
or lovers locked together in drunken lust –
there was nothing we wouldn't do to shock or disgust –

that her mother sat upon the bed, pulling apart dislocated jaws
like some Greek tragedy portraying guilt
and I could see her too, tossing my writings down the bog:
sometimes I thought my lover was a little crazy
the crucifix she made from barbed wire
and some decomposing animal looked good
upon the cupboard door, a nailed barn fox, a good luck hex
but was it art? it made sense, like the Swiss boy below

who wanted to fight in Ireland, God knows
he craved a suicide, I couldn't make him see
that slipping into the grey monotonous estates of Belfast
was like sliding down the inside of a grain silo
into perpetual insanity, it was better to stay where we were

the windows papered over, the crucifix stinking
the little Polish girl who liked to pull me off
the garden below overgrown and used by junkies
as a shit-house by school children:

my lover racked with pain and prescription drugs
yet things it seemed were simpler then
no need to travel beyond a flat land
and Xenophanes has seen the Spartan women doing acrobatics
in the nude, firming-up their breasts, and calls from the kitchenette,
No matter how hard I try to give them reason,
I could never turn them from their Gods.

About the Poet

Gary Allen was born in Ballymena, Co. Antrim. The author of fourteen acclaimed collections, he has been praised throughout Ireland for his honest and gritty poems. His books have been extensively reviewed in major literary magazines and newspapers, earning praise, from among others, from fellow poets Medbh McGuckian, Martin Mooney, Sebastian Barker, Jim Burns, and Alan Gillis. His poems have been widely published in literary magazines throughout Ireland, UK, mainland Europe, USA, Canada, Australia, and New Zealand, such as, *Irish Pages, Poetry Ireland, The Yellow Nib, Ambit, Dark Horse, Edinburgh Review, London Magazine, The Poetry Review, The Reader, Stand, Alaska Quarterly Review, Prairie Schooner, South Carolina Review, The Threepenny Review, Fiddlehead, Malahat Review, Australian Book Review, Meanjin, Poetry NZ,* etc. and many international anthologies of Irish poetry, such as, "The True North," Wake Forest University Press, and in the UK by Salt. An author as well as a poet, he has published three novels and a collection of short stories. Allen has often been described by his peers as one of the most interesting and intriguing of the most-Heaney generation of Irish poets. Now, American readers can decide for themselves with this first published USA edition of his poems. "Mapland," takes us on an inner journey to inherent, if uncomfortable, truths about the world we live in, and ourselves in it.

www.ingramcontent.com/pod-product-compliance
Lightning Source LLC
Chambersburg PA
CBHW020337170426
43200CB00006B/414